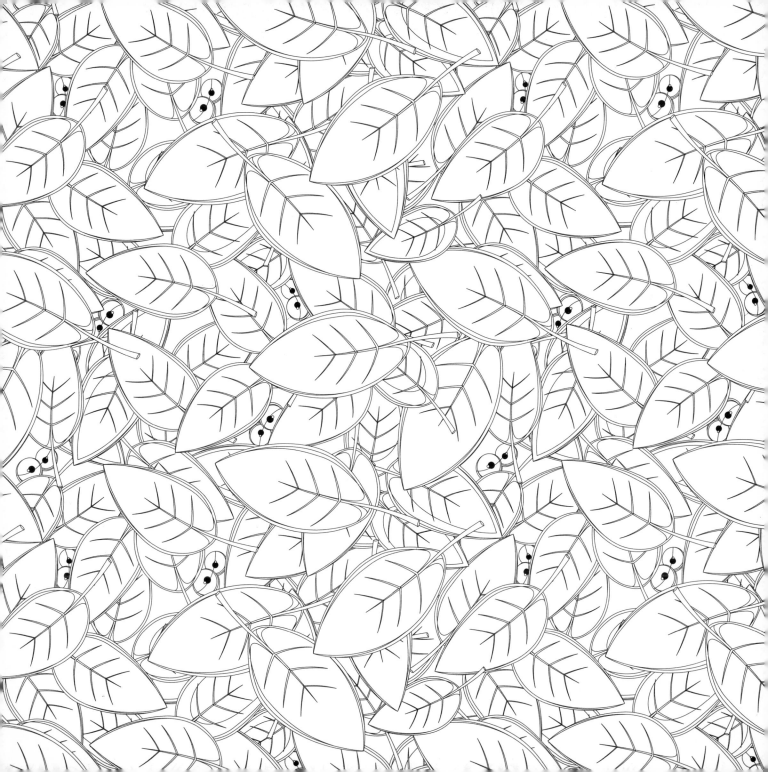

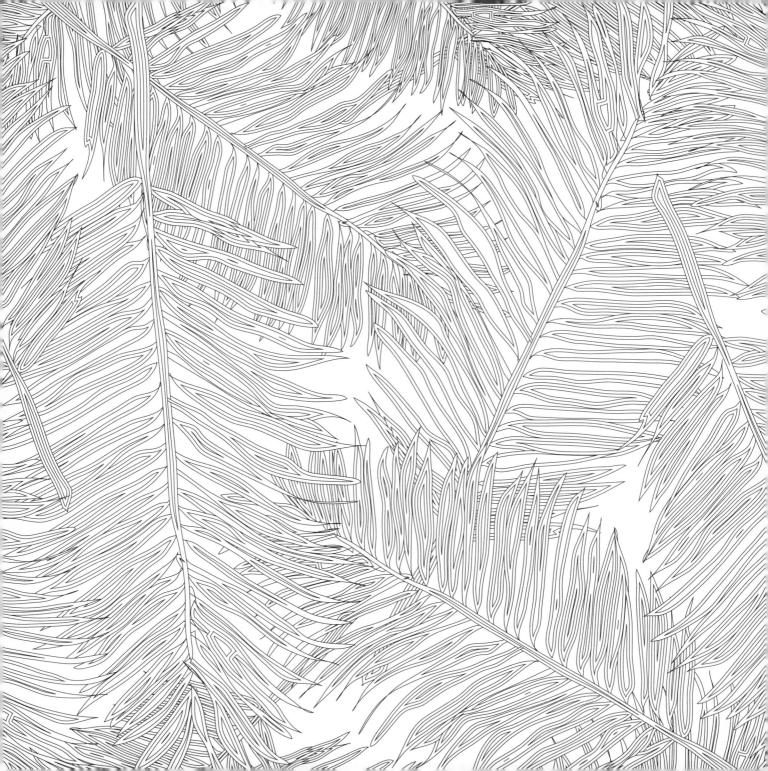

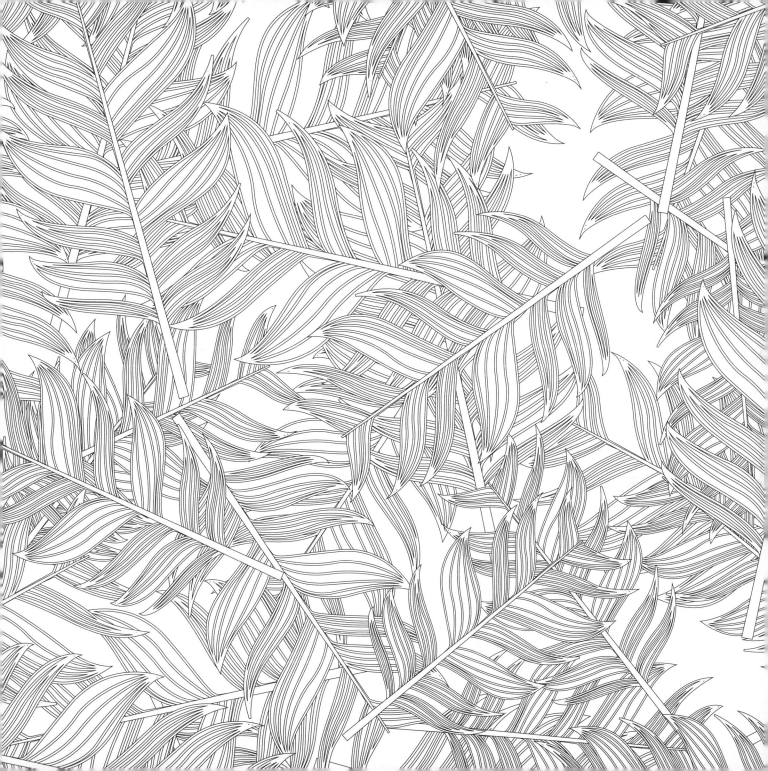

CREDITS

Cover: © Irina Voloshina/Shutterstock.com; © pani/Shutterstock.com
Interior: p. 1: © Artiste : aqua_marinka/istock.com; p. 2: © Lola Tsvetaeva/Shutterstock.com; p. 3: © bekulnis/Shutterstock.com; p. 4: © Andrei Verner/Shutterstock.com; p. 5: © Aqua5/Shutterstock.com; p. 6: © Andrei Verner/Shutterstock.com; p. 7: © moopsi/Shutterstock.com; p. 8: © Maaike Boot/Shutterstock.com; p. 9: Rita Ko/Shutterstock.com; p. 10: © lian_2011/Shutterstock.com; p. 11: © tukkki/Shutterstock.com; p. 12: © smilewithjul/Shutterstock.com; p. 13: © Olga Zakharova/Shutterstock.com; p. 14: © Lola Tsvetaeva/Shutterstock.com; p. 15: © ivgroznii/Shutterstock.com; p. 16: © MariykaA/Shutterstock.com; p. 17: © Dudi/iStock.com; p. 18: © KateVogel/Shutterstock.com; p. 19: © Maria Erypalova/Shutterstock.com; p. 20: © Kynata/Shutterstock.com; p. 21: © Aratehortua/Shutterstock.com; p. 22: © grzhmelek/Shutterstock.com; p. 23: © LenLis/Shutterstock.com; p. 24: © Kozoriz Yuriy/Shutterstock.com; p. 25: © konahinab/Shutterstock.com; p. 26: © viktor vector/Shutterstock.com; p. 27: © bekulnis/Shutterstock.com; p. 28: © karakotsya/Shutterstock.com; p. 29: © balabolka/Shutterstock.com; p. 30: © Tania Anisimova/Shutterstock.com; p. 31: © tets/Shutterstock.com; p. 32: © Markovka/Shutterstock.com; p. 33: © Incomible/Shutterstock.com; p. 34: © bekulnis/Shutterstock.com; p. 35: © Anna Paff/Shutterstock.com; p. 36: © zubarevid/Shutterstock.com; p. 37: © benchart/Shutterstock.com; p. 38: © MariykaA/Shutterstock.com; p. 39: © zolssa/Shutterstock.com; p. 40: © daniana/Shutterstock.com; p. 41: isveta/Shutterstock.com; p. 42: © daniana/Shutterstock.com; p. 43: © Annareichel/Shutterstock.com; p. 44: © Lyusya/Shutterstock.com; p. 45: © Lyusya/Shutterstock.com; p. 46: © Slanapotam/Shutterstock.com; p. 47: © bekulnis/Shutterstock.com; p. 48: © mything/Shutterstock.com; p. 49: © blackstroke/Shutterstock.com; p. 50: © balabolka/Shutterstock.com; p. 51: © Transia Design/Shutterstock.com; p. 52: © Annareichel/Shutterstock.com; p. 53: © smilewithjul/Shutterstock.com; p. 54: © Kozoriz Yuriy/Shutterstock.com; p. 55: © Ashley Mcginty/Shutterstock.com; p. 56: © zolssa/Shutterstock.com; p. 57: © Oliver SIDNEY/Shutterstock.com; p. 58: © ArtHeart/Shutterstock.com; p. 59: © Depiano/Shutterstock.com; p. 60: © paprika/Shutterstock.com; p. 61: © Olga Zakharova/Shutterstock.com; p. 62: © Olga Zakharova /Shutterstock.com; p. 63: © balabolka/Shutterstock.com; p. 64: © Andrei Verner/Shutterstock.com; p. 65: © Andrei Verner/Shutterstock.com; p. 66: © Annareichel/Shutterstock.com; p. 67: © Olga Zakharova/Shutterstock.com; p. 68: © Andrei Verner/Shutterstock.com; p. 69: © Andrei Verner /Shutterstock.com; p. 70: ©Andrei Verner/Shutterstock.com; p. 71: © Andrei Verner/Shutterstock.com; p. 72: © bekulnis/Shutterstock.com.

An Hachette UK Company
www.hachette.co.uk

First published in France in 2014 by Dessain et Tolra

This edition published in Great Britain in 2015 by Hamlyn,
a division of Octopus Publishing Group Ltd
Carmelite House, 50 Victoria Embankment, London EC4Y 0DZ

Copyright © Dessain et Tolra/Larousse 2014
English Translation © Octopus Publishing Group Ltd 2015

Distributed in the US by Hachette Book Group
1290 Avenue of the Americas, 4th and 5th Floors
New York, NY 10020

Distributed in Canada by Canadian Manda Group
664 Annette St., Toronto, Ontario, Canada M6S 2C8

ISBN 978-0-600-63379-2

Printed and bound in China

Publishing directors: Isabelle Jeuge-Maynart, Ghislaine Stora
Editorial direction: Catherine Maillet
Layout: Patrick Leleux PAO
Cover: Claire Morel Fatio, Naomi Edmondson
Senior production manager: Katherine Hockley